FARMING IN THE 1920s AND '30s

Jonathan Brown

First published in Great Britain in 2012 by Shire Publications, part of Bloomsbury Publishing Plc
PO Box 883, Oxford, OX1 9PL, UK
1385 Broadway, 5th Floor, New York, NY 10018, USA
Email: shire@shirebooks.co.uk   www.shirebooks.co.uk

A CIP catalogue record for this book is available from the British Library.

Shire Library No. 666   ISBN-13: 978 0 74781 094 0

Jonathan Brown has asserted his right under the Copyright, Designs and Patents Act, 1988, to be identified as the author of this book.

Designed by Tony Truscott Designs, Sussex, UK
Typeset in Perpetua and Gill Sans.
Printed in China through World Print Ltd.

17 18 19 20 21   11 10 9 8 7 6 5 4 3 2

COVER IMAGE
An advertisement for the Fordson tractor published in 1938, when the tractor was painted bright orange.

TITLE PAGE IMAGE
A young lad drives his wagon past the dairy cows at Mr Denton's farm, East Garston, Berkshire.

CONTENTS PAGE IMAGE
An advertisement for the Hornsby tractor-drawn binder of the 1930s.

ACKNOWLEDGEMENTS
Illustrations are from the collection of the Museum of English Rural Life, Reading.

Shire Publications is supporting the Woodland Trust, the UK's leading woodland conservation charity, by funding the dedication of trees.

CONTENTS

INTRODUCTION

T HE DECADES between the two world wars were a time of contrasts. It was an age of economic difficulty, of industrial depression, strikes in the coal mines, unemployment and international insecurity. Yet there were many new, sometimes exciting developments: radio, dance bands and new consumer goods made in trading estates on new arterial roads along which motor cars and lorries travelled. The 1930s brought not only dole queues, but also a new age of elegance – of streamlined design, aviation and fast trains.

There was increased leisure time for some as well, enabling many town-dwellers to visit the countryside. Enticed by railway posters, perhaps, or guide-books with their attractive covers, people came to enjoy a ramble or picnic among picturesque hills, dales and villages. The visitors perhaps saw an idyllic countryside, but life in the village and on the farm was as full of contrasts as everywhere else. Hopes of the dawning of a new age after the First World War were quickly dashed, and farmers returned to their struggle with challenging economic conditions. For them, hard work continued as before – the daily round of milking, carting feed to cattle in wintry fields, and doing battle with markets unwilling to pay a good price for their produce.

There were new things for the farmer – new markets for sugar beet, eggs, milk and pork. Many new machines were introduced, although few farmers could afford them until well into the 1930s. The motor car and lorry arrived on the farm. Some of the comforts of urban life were reaching villages and farms. The arrival of mains water made a big impact. When the mains reached Brightman's Farm in Pinchbeck, Lincolnshire, in 1935, it brought about a major change to life in the farmhouse. No longer did drinking water have to come from tanks that stored rainwater, which had to be filtered through charcoal to make it usable.

While the countryside might have seemed unchanging, the effect of all these influences was that the nature of the inter-war farm was becoming quite different from its Victorian and Edwardian predecessors.

Opposite:
The type of rural scene to attract the visitors: thatched cottages in St Mary Bourne, Hampshire.

ADJUSTING TO PEACE IN THE 1920s

A FTER THE First World War English agriculture suffered a severe shock. War always places particular demands on the farmer. It disrupts and distorts patterns of activity established in peacetime. It forces up the prices of agricultural commodities that have become scarce, especially those that have been imported. It creates a shortage of labour and increases its cost. All of these difficulties were experienced to an unprecedented extent in the First World War – what many have called the first 'total war'.

Pressure to feed the nation at war brought about government involvement in agriculture in ways not experienced before. The state took control of the markets, setting upper limits to prices, but also offering to maintain minimum prices for two commodities – wheat and oats. It intervened in the labour market, setting minimum wages and helping with the supply of labour through the employment of prisoners of war and the new Women's Land Army. It told farmers what they should be producing – cereals and potatoes, which had greater immediate calorific value as human food than the meat and milk that farmers had been finding more profitable before the war. Local war agricultural committees were appointed to oversee the implementation of this policy, leading to the phrase 'farming from Whitehall' entering the farmer's lexicon of abuse. Exhortation and manipulation of markets turned to direction, with the introduction of the ploughing-up campaign in 1917 to force farmers to turn more of their grassland over to cereals. The campaign's success can be measured in the 1.4 million acres of pasture that were ploughed up between 1916 and 1918.

After the war there was talk of creating new stability for agriculture. 'We must have a settled policy with regard to agriculture,' said Lloyd George, the Prime Minister, in 1919. Farmers' leaders generally agreed, assuming that what was meant was a continuation of the wartime minimum price guarantees that would support the arable farmer. A new Agriculture Act was passed in 1920 to put that into effect.

It could not and did not last. The government soon realised that it could not afford to underwrite the price of cereals as world market prices started

Opposite: According to this detail from an advertisement, Bibby's animal feed apparently made every farmer as prosperous as this one seems to be.

to fall, with the prospect that they would drop well below the guaranteed minima. The Agriculture Act was repealed in 1921 before the government had to pay any of the bills in support of cereal prices, an episode that went down in farming's folk history as the 'Great Betrayal'.

This was when the pain of adjustment to peacetime economics began to be felt in earnest, and it set the tone for the next two decades. Markets were now free, overseas trade was restored, bringing imports back to pre-war volumes, and prices for agricultural produce generally fell. Wheat was trading at 10–12s a hundredweight during the 1920s, compared to its wartime height of 15–17s, and it fell further after the economic crash of 1929. Wool fell sharply in price – by three-quarters for Southdown wool – and most other prices in the 1920s were about a third less than they had been in wartime. Even though there might be fluctuations from year to year and differences in experience from one farmer to another, the general feeling was that agriculture was in a state of depression.

Yet life on the farm survived. Profits were hard to come by – a combination of low prices and increased costs placed constant pressure on the farmer's budget. Arable farming was hit the hardest. George Baylis had been one of the great successes of Edwardian farming. He had built up an extensive

Opposite top:
Cart teams being led out on Notgrove Farm, Gloucestershire, in 1920.

Opposite bottom:
Haughley Farm, Suffolk, home of Lady Balfour, one of the founders of the modern organic movement.

A competitor at the Hertfordshire hedging competition in 1936. Tending hedges by hand was something many farmers could not afford.

9

Major V. S. Bland of Aldbourne, Wiltshire, who turned his farm into a 'hive of industry'.

Instead of hedges, wire fencing was becoming more attractive as an efficient way of restraining stock.

farming enterprise on the downlands of Berkshire, where he succeeded in the profitable cultivation of wheat at low cost. After the war things turned against him. Whereas he had been able to make a profit from wheat at 7s 6d a hundredweight before 1914, in the 1920s he was losing money on wheat at 12s a hundredweight (some prices in the 1920s were higher than pre-war). The difference was that his costs, and especially labour costs, had increased disproportionately, from 50s an acre for his tillage operations in 1908–10 to more than £4 an acre twenty years later.

With costs often exceeding income, farmers found themselves in a vicious cycle: with capital draining away, they could not afford to invest in

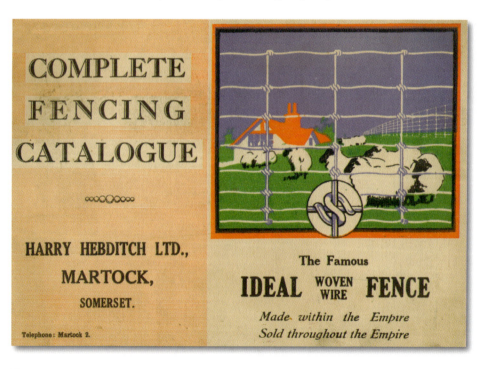

COMPLETE FENCING CATALOGUE

HARRY HEBDITCH LTD., MARTOCK, SOMERSET.

Telephone: Martock 2.

The Famous

IDEAL WOVEN WIRE FENCE

Made within the Empire
Sold throughout the Empire

labour-saving and cost-saving implements and techniques. For many the struggle became too much. The accounts of a small farmer in North Yorkshire show losses mounting as prices for his stock fell, while the money he was laying out on feed changed relatively little. From a healthy balance of £1,670 in 1919 he was down to £163 in two years. He gave up his farm in 1923. So did thousands of others in the 1920s and early 1930s.

Despite these difficulties, farmers continued, as they had in previous years, to adjust to the circumstances of the times. The *Farmers Weekly* was first published in 1934, despite what might have seemed to be unpropitious times for a new venture, and soon established itself as one of the leading newspapers for the farming industry. Among its long-running features was a series on 'Successful Farmers', which focused attention on some of those farmers who were doing well in difficult times. The key to all their success was an ability to adapt their farming methods, and the adoption of new techniques and tools. Where this was happening, farming could even be said to be thriving in the 1930s, and by the end of the decade considerable changes had taken place on the farm compared with the early 1920s.

Modern Art Deco design was used for advertising Albion harvesting machinery. This mower is from a catalogue issued in 1934.

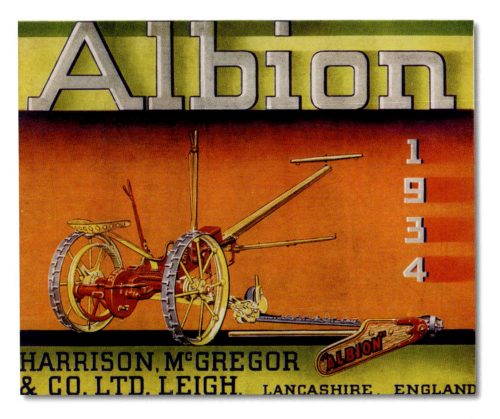

THE FARMERS

To see a gathering of farmers on market day in the 1920s would give the impression that little had changed since before the First World War. There they would be, leaning on the rails of the stock pens, comparing the points of the animals just as in times past. No wonder advertisers found this such a good image to evoke solidity and dependability. The farmers were not always looking as jolly as the one in Bibby's advertisement: photographs tend to show them looking far more serious as they contemplate the stock and the price, which was, naturally, never as high as they hoped.

The impression given by this view of the market place was accurate only in parts, for, of course, much had changed in farming life during and after the war. For a start, the people themselves were changing with each successive year. Some of them had been farming before 1914, but the generations were passing, bringing in new blood. A. G. Street had succeeded his father on his farm in Wiltshire. The change from father to son was a common enough happening, but turnover in the farming population was unusually high from other causes. Movement in and out of farming during the inter-war years was considerable, probably greater than in previous periods, and certainly more than in later times. Sons had been lost in the war, while recession after the war forced many to leave farming.

New people came in their place, so that it is quite common to find someone in farming today whose grandfather or great-grandfather was the one who first took the family farm in the 1920s. The result of this fresh intake was that in total the numbers of farmers changed little between the world wars: despite all the talk of depression in farming, prospects seemed sufficiently good to attract the newcomers. The low price of land, whether to rent or buy, was another incentive for the new farmer.

The new farmers of the 1920s came with a wide range of experience. Many, probably most, came from families with some connection with the land, but they were not all farmers' sons. Many seized opportunities that opened up for them on demobilisation from the forces. Some relatives of farmers and men who had been labourers before the war were able to take a county council smallholding to set them on the farming ladder. W. H. Owen was from a farming family in Lincolnshire; he had moved to Australia before the war, but, after wartime service in the Australian army, he returned to Lincolnshire and took the 120-acre Bridge End Farm at Horbling in 1920. The officer class was also well represented: majors and captains seemed at times to be everywhere, some of them sons of the farm returning to the land, others coming in fresh to the industry. In reality they were a small minority of the farming population: perhaps the farming magazines visited them more often. General Adlercron was one of these army officers; he started as a dairy farmer just after the First World War and built up a business selling milk to Nottingham and other towns in the neighbourhood, investing heavily in modern methods.

Like W. H. Owen, A. G. Street spent a few years overseas as a young man. He went to Canada, gaining experience on a farm in Winnipeg before returning to his family's farm in Wiltshire. He was not unusual in this: time

A cattle market scene in the 1922 calendar of Bibby's, the feed millers.

Above: Friesian cattle graze in a field, with farmhouse and silo beyond, on E. G. Barton's farm at Saundby, near Retford, Nottinghamshire, 1930.

Right: An animated scene at a calf sale in Epping market, Essex, in April 1939.

in Canada, Australia, South or East Africa was almost a rite of passage for some farming sons.

There was an unusually large number of women entering farming on their own account. They were mostly single, farming being thought a suitable occupation for women of good class. They made up a very small proportion of the total number of farmers, but there were enough of them to make an impact, and *Farmer and Stockbreeder* ran a series on 'Successful Women Farmers', in competition with *Farmers Weekly*, which had featured only men in its series.

As well as the new generation of men and women gathering in the market place, the market itself was changing. The telephone and the motor lorry had entered the farmer's life and were changing the way he did business. A few telephone conversations with the grain merchant could secure a deal, and a lorry would take a delivery straight to the mill; there was no need to go to the market to sell the wheat. As a result corn exchanges were starting to close. The same combination of telephone and motor lorry was just as effective in enabling the development of new businesses and their marketing, such as the supply of eggs and vegetables, and the regular collection of milk from the farm. The livestock market was still there, but here also the lorry and the telephone were having an effect, leading to the closure of some small markets and fairs.

Miss Harrison Bell, one of the women who took up farming in the inter-war period. On her farm at Codicote, Hertfordshire, she specialised in ducks and poultry for the table at a time when this was unusual.

Along with the new people engaged in farming, the passing generations introduced new attitudes. To cope with the difficult economic environment, a farmer had to be meticulous in his record-keeping. The farms run by P. Webster Cory at Notgrove in Gloucestershire were celebrated at the time as an example of good business organisation. He had started farming in 1916 on a purely arable farm, but converted it into an enterprise based on grass and built it up to 1,000 acres in extent. He managed his farm in four departments for accounting purposes – dairy, poultry, pigs and sheep – rather like a manufacturing company. Such practices were not confined to the large, well-known farmers. A good set of accounts was one of the principal means that new Lincolnshire farmer W. H. Owen used to keep in the black and stay in farming throughout this period. Other practices were adopted from the industrial and commercial world, such as the incorporation of farm businesses with limited liability.

It was often the newcomers to farming – like Owen – who were the first to adopt new business

A lorry of around First World War vintage being loaded with sacks on the farm of White & Son in Somerset, in March 1931. Through the top window of the barn the wheel of a chaff-cutter can be glimpsed.

practices. They had the incentive of wanting to keep the capital they had brought into the farm, and some brought new dynamism to carry farming through difficult times – taking advantage of low costs, especially of land, to build up a business. Ralph Godfrey was one of these new farmers. He started farming in 1918 with 140 acres at Melton Ross, Lincolnshire. By 1939 he had built up his holdings to 3,500 acres.

The farmer of the 1920s and 1930s was more likely to be an owner of his land than his counterpart before the First World War. Immediately after the war many estates took advantage of high prices to sell some of their land, sometimes all of it. Turnover in landownership was great in some areas: in Oxfordshire two-thirds of gentry estates changed hands. The tenant farmers were often foremost among the purchasers – from a sense of self-protection as much as anything. With members of the traditional landowning class rarely in the market, farmers preferred to buy rather than risk an unknown new landlord, even though they would be saddled with a mortgage. The result of these sales was that, whereas before 1914 about 10 per cent of farmland was owner-occupied, much of that accounted for by the estate's home farms, by 1927 more than a third of the agricultural land of England and Wales was owner-occupied. Those who came new to farming after 1918 were more likely to invest in a freehold farm.

Another outcome of the land sales was a change in the relationship between farmer and landowner, and indeed between farmer and village society. The farmer was a landowner now, often on the scale of the lesser gentry. Meanwhile, some of the established landowners had turned themselves into more active land managers, including farming a high proportion of their estates. The Neviles, one of Lincolnshire's old landowning families, became progressive farmers during this period, and one of their neighbours, Lord Londesborough, formed the farms managed by his estate into a limited company. Referring to the late nineteenth century, Somerset Maugham wrote in *Of Human Bondage* that 'a fine distinction was made between the gentleman farmer and the landowner'. Those distinctions were no less fine between the landowning farmer and the working estate owner.

The narrowing of the gap between farmer and landowner meant that leaders of the agricultural world were no longer drawn exclusively from the landowners, but were as likely to come from the farming class, especially now that the National Farmers' Union had established itself as a dominant pressure group. For the farmer had joined the era of collective organisation: he had his union, the National Farmers' Union, to speak on his behalf to governments and other parties. The union had been founded in 1908 and had soon established itself as a lobbying organisation, especially during the war. Its membership increased steadily: in 1909, six months after the union's formation, there were already ten thousand members; by 1930 there were

Manual labour is still much in evidence in this scene of stack-building.

112,000. Another mark of its success was the appointment of Major Reginald Dorman-Smith, a past president of the union, as Minister of Agriculture in 1938. The foundation of the NFU did not make the farmers any more homogeneous as a group. To many farmers, the NFU was regarded as a club for the large farmers of eastern and southern England. The disgruntled from time to time established other organisations for small farmers, dairy farmers or other interest groups.

For the farmer keeping a close eye on his set of accounts, the greatest concern was the cost of labour. Arable farming caused especial concern, with its preponderance of manual work in the 1920s. After wartime controls were lifted in 1921, farmers tried hard to reduce their labour costs, including cutting wages. They often succeeded, but at the cost of bitterness amongst their workers. Widespread strikes in 1923 were settled generally in the farmer's favour, but the disputes prompted government to reintroduce wage controls in 1924. With the matter of wages taken out of the farmers' hands (much to their annoyance), relations with the workers gradually settled down. That did not end the pressure to keep costs down, and the numbers of labourers declined throughout the inter-war years. This was a relatively slow process during the 1920s: the number of regular labourers in England and Wales declined in that decade from 685,000 in 1921 to 644,000 in 1929. The pace of change increased during the 1930s, partly the effect of greater mechanisation, and the total came down to 511,000 in 1939.

Two Fordson tractors at work in the fields of A. C. Moore's farm in Leicestershire, July 1933.

THE FARMS

Eᴺɢʟɪsʜ ᴀɢʀɪᴄᴜʟᴛᴜʀᴇ had a long-established tradition of mixed farming, and it continued into the inter-war years. J. W. Pye was a proud upholder of that tradition. He had a farm of 636 acres at Cuxton, near Rochester in Kent, which he had acquired in 1911, buying the freehold in 1926. He had a balance of crops and livestock. Most of the land was under arable cropping, growing cereals – especially malting barley, potatoes, vegetables, hops, and fodder crops for the livestock. There was a flock of 170 ewes and some cattle, and in 1936, when he was interviewed by *Farmer and Stockbreeder*, he was trying his hand at poultry. The work on the land was done by twelve horses and two tractors, with twenty-four men regularly employed.

There were many more farmers like Pye, but there was a growing trend towards concentrating on one or two lines rather than spreading the business risks over a wide range of crops and stock. Captain E. T. Morris, the president of the National Farmers Union in 1930, farmed on a similar scale to Pye, having 500 acres in Hertfordshire. In many ways his farm was also a typical mixed farm. He kept nearly four-fifths of the land in arable cultivation, and he had sheep and cattle. But the reality of his business was that he was a cattle farmer – they earned the money. Most of his money came from the sale of fatstock for beef from his pedigree herd of Lincoln Red Shorthorn cattle – an unusual choice for his district, but a breed that gave him the quality he wanted. A small dairy herd of the same breed yielded the second main line of income. Everything else on this farm was secondary to these.

Spraying apple trees at Harwell, now in Oxfordshire.

Some of Captain Morris's Lincoln Red cattle in Hertfordshire, 1930.

Unloading cattle at J. D. Evans's farm, Upton Magna, Shropshire, April 1933.

William Todd, of Little Ponton Grange in south Lincolnshire, was another man who had a farm mixed in general appearance, on which he kept sheep and cattle. In fact he was a specialist breeder of livestock. Almost all his animals were of pedigree stock. In 1935 he had seven hundred to a thousand Hampshire Down sheep, and sixty to eighty Shorthorn cattle; he also had fifty Shire horses. He regularly won prizes at the agricultural shows, boosting his prestige and sales, which he made throughout the world.

There had been specialist farmers before, of course, whether small-scale dairy farmers or large-scale cereal growers, such as George Baylis. There had also been farmers with specialities within mixed farming before, but times had changed so much that few of the former certainties could be relied upon. Major Bland, one of the 'Successful Farmers', had 2,250 acres mostly on the chalk downs at Aldbourne, Wiltshire. Before the First World War the farm had been simply a corn and sheep enterprise, in common with many downland farms. Now, said the *Farmers Weekly*, it was 'a hive of industry with milking cows, sheep, pigs and poultry contributing towards the production of wheat, oats and barley'. Major Bland had had to reassess the structure of his farming and think afresh about what his main lines of produce would be. Most farmers did, and for most the choice settled on livestock.

Rabbits had become a serious pest on farms by the 1930s. Some are being treated to carbon monoxide poison on the farm of C. J. Barton, Welwyn, Hertfordshire, in 1933.

COWS, PIGS AND SHEEP

THE SITUATIONS VACANT columns in the weekly farming magazines, *Farmer and Stockbreeder* and *Farmers Weekly*, were dominated by advertisements for cowmen, stockmen, pigmen and farm bailiffs. It was an unrepresentative sample because general labouring posts were filled without advertising in the national press, but it demonstrates the importance that skills had in twentieth-century farming. They were sought after, and those possessing them were often prepared to move to jobs around the country. These particular skills were in demand because livestock represented the best source of profit for most farmers of the 1920s and 1930s. Farmers everywhere turned to cattle, sheep and pigs – in the arable eastern counties as much as in the pastoral west. By the early 1930s research at the University of Cambridge showed that two-thirds of farm income in the eastern counties came from sales of livestock.

In a sense farmers had been here before. Conditions before 1914 had generally favoured livestock, so farmers set about recreating pre-war conditions, in some respects at least. One of these was the use of pasture land. Although Captain Morris, who was farming prime wheat land, kept a high proportion of his farm in arable cultivation, this was not something that most farmers wanted to do. Arable was expensive, especially in labour, and, with weak markets for most arable products, it was not cost-effective, even in support of a livestock farm. It was often cheaper for the farmer to buy prepared livestock feeds than grow his own, and, therefore, the roots rotation of turnips and swedes, which required weeding and singling, was avoided. Instead, temporary pastures and grass grown in rotation for hay were a better proposition. Permanent pasture was also more important, gradually increasing in extent each year throughout the 1920s, until by the 1930s it was the same as it had been in the Edwardian years at about 15.8 million acres. The simple reason for this was that pasture took hardly any costly labour to keep up: no sowing, weeding and tending; merely, perhaps, some top-dressing with fertiliser.

The importance that grassland had assumed was enough to prompt the establishment of research centres studying methods of improving pastures

Opposite:
Feeding young
stock in the field
on a cold winter
day.

23

Two farm workers and two bullocks of the beef herd of G. Blair, who farmed at Upleatham, North Yorkshire.

and meadows. Sir George Stapledon at Aberystwyth started his experimental work on the composition of pastures in 1919; by the mid-1930s his findings were beginning to make a contribution to improvement in farm practice, especially on hill-farm pastures.

Of the main branches of livestock farming, cattle were the most common: most farmers kept at least a few cattle. In all, the number of cattle grew by 22 per cent between 1920 and 1939. The number of specialist workers with cows was also kept up: there was a decline in the farm-working population between the censuses of 1911 and 1931, but numbers of cowmen fell by only 9.8 per cent, compared with the 21.2 per cent decline in general workers. Dairy farming accounted for a high proportion of the increase in numbers of cattle: the strength of the dairy sector was so great that it merits a separate chapter.

While both the beef and dairy branches of cattle farming expanded, there was a sharp divide between the two. Captain Morris, who kept his Lincoln Reds for both meat and milk, was getting out of step with the times, as farmers increasingly were concentrating on one or the other. Consequently dual-purpose breeds fell out of favour, especially the Shorthorns, which had been the mainstay of cattle farming for a long time. Their place was taken by specialist breeds: beef producers concentrated on such breeds as the Hereford, and dairymen on high milk yielders, especially the Friesian.

Frequently appearing among the job advertisements in the *Farmers Weekly* was the pigman. He and his pigs could be said to have been among the main beneficiaries of the growth of livestock farming in the 1920s and 1930s.

Choosing the next lot of fat cattle for market in the strawyard at G. Weston's farm near Norwich, November 1934.

Keeping pigs had been one of the least important of the branches of farming, but now numbers of pigs shot up from 1,994,000 in 1920 to 3,515,000 in 1939, an increase of 76.3 per cent.

Beef stock in the yard on E. W. K. Slade's farm, Compton, Berkshire. A group of onlookers has gathered on the other side of the wall, January 1931.

'An investment' – or so Lawes Chemicals claimed for their cattle spray in the 1930s.

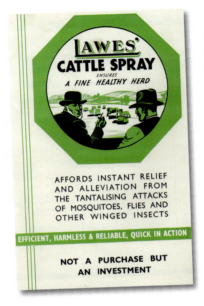

A sow and piglets in their own field enclosure on a farm at Watford in Northamptonshire, 1938.

Pigs had rarely been treated as a serious part of farming, but rather as a useful adjunct, eating scraps, supplying the household with meat and providing some extra income. They had always been something of a speciality in some areas – Lincolnshire, for example. But even there they had generally been regarded as a sideshow. This meant they were rarely farmed systematically, so that their numbers fluctuated greatly from year to year, a consequence of their short gestation period. Some farmers had started to take pigs more seriously at the end of the nineteenth century, but there were few of them and the effect on the number of pigs had been small. Now, however, there was real growth as more farmers realised the benefits of making pigs one of their specialisms, not just a sideline. This was what B. H. Baron-Clarke did on his farm at Haskerton Hall, Suffolk. 'Pigs fitted into my scheme of farming – there is

no better manure for the fruit trees,' he told the *Farmer and Stockbreeder*. But he had to take them seriously and accord them status as a proper department in his farming. To make a profit from them, he needed to produce the best quality bacon.

With the growth of pig farming, pigs were to be found almost everywhere, on large farms and small, in lowlands and on the hills, for they could be incorporated into almost any style of farming. While Baron-Clarke kept his pigs alongside fruit, others kept them with a dairy herd, with poultry, or as part of a mixed stock and arable farm. Most pigs were kept as one important string to the farmer's bow, but there were a number of specialist pig farms by the 1930s. Captain J. H. Grant was one of the specialists, keeping pigs on the hill pastures of the farm at Winscombe, Somerset, that he bought in 1934.

Pig-keeping could be a risky proposition, with fluctuations in price quickly reflected in numbers. But the market was expanding, and, encouraged especially by stability under marketing schemes for bacon and pigs, some farmers found it worth putting in the effort of management. Some

B. H. Baron-Clarke was not the only farmer to keep pigs alongside fruit. These pigs beneath springtime blossom were in Berkshire.

New products, such as this potato masher, were available for the new age of pig farming.

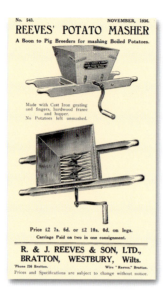

No. 543.   NOVEMBER, 1936.

REEVES' POTATO MASHER
A Boon to Pig Breeders for mashing Boiled Potatoes.

Made with Cast Iron grating and fingers, hardwood frame and hopper.
No Potatoes left unmashed.

Price £2 7s. 6d. or £2 10s. 0d. on legs.
Carriage Paid on two in one consignment.

**R. & J. REEVES & SON, LTD.,
BRATTON, WESTBURY, Wilts.**
'Phone 236 Bratton.   Wire "Reeves," Bratton.
Prices and Specifications are subject to change without notice.

of the risks were mitigated by concentrating on a few breeds. The Large White became by far the most common breed of the time, while the Large Black and the Berkshire were also popular.

While the situations vacant columns in the farming magazines included several advertisements for specialist workmen with cattle and pigs, there were far fewer for shepherds. Indeed, the number of shepherds fell by almost a half between 1911 and 1931. Yet the total number of sheep increased between 1920 and 1939, to reach nearly 18 million. The way the sheep were kept, however, changed considerably. One of the big changes was that the 'sheep-corn' system of farming on the mixed farms of southern England was no longer economical. This was the system practised on A. G. Street's farm in Wiltshire until he found the labour required to manage sheep feeding on

Feeding pigs at Ipsden, Oxfordshire.

Large flocks of sheep grazing on the downs of Wiltshire were becoming a less common sight when this photograph was taken in May 1937.

fodder crops was too great. Street turned to dairying; others opted to keep their sheep on grass. Either way, it meant that the shepherd on the downs was a less common sight by the 1930s.

It was not only on the downs that such changes occurred. Almost everywhere the preference was for keeping sheep mainly on grass, whether in Kent, in the Cotswolds or on the hill farms of the north and Wales. With grassland feeding came grassland breeds. Many of the breeds developed for the conditions of lowland mixed arable farms – the Lincolnshire Longwool and the Cotswold, for example – were becoming rare by the end of the 1930s. In their place came Hampshire Down and, especially, Leicester sheep fed on grass, while hardy hill sheep, such as the Cheviot, and cross-breeds, were increasingly kept on lowland grass. They needed less attention as well, hence fewer shepherds.

Shepherds on the downs of Wiltshire, standing beside their mobile hut, May 1937.

Sheep were a mainstay on the hill farms of northern and south-western England and of Wales. In some respects hill farmers could cope well with the difficult economic times. They simply beat a retreat: 'when prices are low, we simply let land drop out of cultivation, and when they improve we take it back again into a kind of provisional cultivation,' wrote a leading Welsh agriculturalist. Many hill farmers did just that during the 1920s, and there were many comments on the deteriorating condition of upland pastures. It meant,

Sheep shearers used clippers powered by oil engine or electricity more frequently in the 1920s and 1930s. This is the head of a Lister powered clipper.

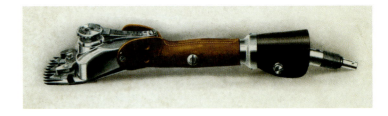

however, that the farmer was left eking out an existence, and there was a limit to how far this way of life could go.

By the 1930s hill farmers were adapting to some of the trends of the age. They were keeping more ewes, so that they could increase their turnover of lambs. If he had pastures good enough, the upland farmer would bring the lambs on over summer and sell to the butcher. Otherwise he sold young lambs to lowland farmers to fatten. Some farmers were like the Isaac brothers, who farmed on the hills above the Rhondda; they were confident enough in the late 1930s to start improving their pastures along the lines of Sir George Stapledon's research findings. They kept Welsh Mountain ewes on the improved hill pastures, and dairy cattle on the lower part of the farm.

On a bright summer's day in the Cotswolds in the 1920s, sheep shearers seek shade to clip the sheep by hand.

Not every farmer had the sea in which to wash his sheep. This scene is at Llanbedrog, North Wales.

Early-morning rounding up of sheep in the Welsh hills near Llangollen.

DAIRY FARMING

WHEN HE ENTERED FARMING on his own account after his father died in 1918, A. G. Street carried on with more or less the type of mixed farming he had grown up with, but by 1927 it was clearly not paying. Something had to be done, and Street's course was to go into dairy farming.

It was a bold move because it required a major change to his farming practices. He had grown up with a mainly arable farm, and now he was going to put most of that land down to grass – on the Wiltshire Downs, which were not obviously suited to cow-keeping. Even though livestock had always been

An advertising artist's view of a farm dairy, with the farmer watching while the cream separator is turned, in 1925.

Filling the feed troughs in the cattle sheds on the farm of L. J. Evans at Tittensor, Staffordshire, March 1931.

Modern milking by hand in 1934, at the farm of Miss Andrew in Chalvington, Sussex.

kept on the farm, the change from a mixed farm to a mainly dairy farm involved a new routine of work in the daily milking and the management of the calving. The men who worked with Street on the farm had to change as well.

It was a step that many a farmer had already taken, even in places like this.

The late-Victorian and Edwardian farmers had been turning to milk as one of the most secure and profitable branches of husbandry, and after the war the trend continued. Milk production in England and Wales rose by 24 per cent between 1924–5 and 1934–5, by which time 45 per cent of the cattle kept in Britain were dairy cows.

A. G. Street put a lot of his land down to grass because keeping the cattle out in the field and buying additional feed required little labour and was cheaper than maintaining an arable rotation, even to grow fodder. Investment in buildings could be kept to a minimum, especially if milking was done in the field. Street used milking machines, but in the 1920s most farmers still milked by hand. When General Adlercron adopted machine milking on his Culverthorpe dairy farm immediately after the war he was something of a pioneer. It was not until the 1930s that many farmers looked more seriously at milking machines. For Street, machine milking was integral to another innovation he adopted, the outdoor mobile milking parlour – or 'bail' – the use of which cut out the work of bringing the cows into the yard twice a day, and the expense of a fixed building.

A. J. Hosier, another farmer on the Wiltshire downland, was the man behind the bail system of dairying. It looked rather spartan compared with General Adlercron's gleaming milking parlour – little more than a caravan parked in the field – but Hosier claimed huge savings by its use. His bails for sixty cows could be operated by two men only, and there were other savings, such as the need to clean out and replenish hay and straw in permanent

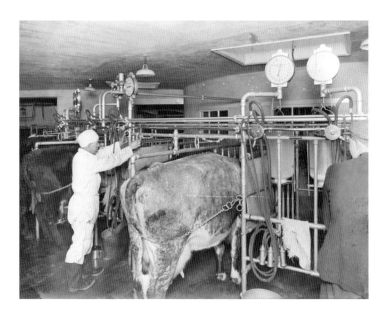

Milking by machine at Culverthorpe Dairy Farm, near Grantham, Lincolnshire. This is Alfa-Laval equipment in use in 1935.

Grassmillees Salome, champion Ayrshire cow at the Shropshire Show in 1934. She was owned by L. K. Osmond of Netherwood Dairy Farm, Bradley, Grimsby, Lincolnshire.

milking sheds. There was no carting of muck out to the fields, since the cows were already there. It was, however, a specialised system particularly suited to large farms on the downlands – Hosier himself had 1,000 acres. It was therefore only a small minority of farmers who converted to Hosier's method – 192 of them, according to a count in 1940. Those who adopted the outdoor bail usually found it worked well for their type of farming, and many kept them at work until the 1960s.

The simple shelter used with a Hosier milking bail on the Webster Cory farms at Notgrove, Gloucestershire.

Increased productivity was one of the features of the dairy farming of this period. By the 1930s cows yielding 1,000 gallons per lactation were becoming common. The average yield per cow reached 539 gallons per lactation by 1934–5, compared with 416 gallons ten years previously. The first cow to yield 3,000 gallons achieved the feat in 1922, and by 1930 there were nine claiming such a figure.

These cows with very high milk yields were all prize pedigree animals, and many farmers concentrated on pedigree stock. E. G. Barton, who farmed at Saundby, Nottinghamshire, was one of them: he reckoned that the fourteen pedigree cows he kept in 1930 were producing as much milk as the twenty-four run-of-the-mill cows he had kept six years before. He kept Friesians, and he was still unusual in choosing this breed, but it was making headway against such breeds as the Dairy Shorthorn. It was not enough to make it the dominant breed yet, but the number of farmers who concentrated their efforts on it was increasing. Pedigree cows were not essential to success: being more meticulous about their stock and being more prepared to buy from specialist breeders was enough to enable most farmers to raise the standard of their herds and yields. Roland Stearn, who kept dairy cows on an arable farm near Stowmarket, Suffolk, followed this path. By being selective about the animals he bought and equally strict about culling cows with low yields, he was able to get an average yield of 1,200 gallons per cow.

The best living to be made in dairy farming was in selling liquid milk. Demand was reasonably strong and the price kept up better than most

Friesian cows in a meadow at East Garston, Berkshire.

Bottling milk in
the farm dairy on
A. Barclay's farm
at Compton,
Berkshire, 1928.

products – it was 16d per gallon in 1922–3 and still 14¼d per gallon in
1927–8. Even though milk joined in the general fall of prices after 1929, it
fell by less than cereals and meat, making the balance in its favour even better.
The milk price was always higher than that for cheese or butter, which could
be undercut by imports. It was the importance of liquid milk that provided
the impetus for raising the productivity of dairy cows. Dairying for milk
required good, consistent yield, whereas greater variability could be accepted
for cheese and butter production.

Another big advantage of dairy farming was that it suited almost all scales
of farming. Hosier and Street each had several hundred acres, but a large
farm and herds were not essential in the 1920s and 1930s. The traditional
dairying counties of the West Country and north were dominated by small
farmers, and this continued to be so. When the Milk Marketing Board was
established, three-quarters of the producers registered with it supplied no
more than 30 gallons a year. The regular cheque for milk was especially
valuable to the small farmers because it freed them from the burden of
producing butter or cheese. It, therefore, represented a considerable saving
of labour, for farmers on this scale relied almost exclusively on family labour,
which did not enter the account record.

The milk market was competitive, however. In the 1920s most farmers
were selling to the big dairy companies, such as Express and United Dairies,
and there were complaints about their use of market muscle to drive prices

Milk churns waiting on a roadside loading platform – a common sight with the advent of milk collection by lorry.

Miss Bowen-Colthurst was featured in *Farmer and Stockbreeder*'s 'Successful Women Farmers' series in April 1932. She had a dairy farm at Layer de la Haye, Essex, and the farm had its own shop in nearby Colchester. Here a van is being loaded with a delivery.

down. Quite a few farmers opted to run their own retailing business, with shops and milk rounds. For this to be successful, urban markets reasonably close by were needed. The small farmer could not emulate Lord Rayleigh, whose estate had a successful wholesale and retail business in the London area supplied from farms in Essex.

The Milk Marketing Board for England and Wales was set up in 1933 under the Agricultural Marketing Acts passed in 1931 and 1933. These Acts were part of the government's response to another downturn in the

agricultural economy following the crash of 1929, the idea being to strengthen the power of the farmer in the market place. The Milk Marketing Board was by far the most successful of the boards established under this legislation. Its ability to set a guaranteed wholesale price, regardless of where the farm was and the use to which the milk was put, made the attraction of milk production even greater. Farmers were generally better off selling the milk rather than going to the trouble of making butter or cheese. Instead, most cheese and butter was now processed in factories and creameries rather than on the farm.

A few of the large dairy farmers who had been able to hold their own in the metropolitan markets were dissatisfied with the new arrangements, but for most farmers the stable market and pricing regime under the board were a godsend. The regular milk cheque from the board quickly became a fact of farming life. Milk production increased in response as the dairy herd grew at a rate faster than it had during the 1920s. The number of producers registered with the board increased from 80,000 to 102,000 in the first five years of its existence. Most of these were small and medium-scale producers, and many were in relatively remote areas, such as Cumbria and North Yorkshire. The stability of the board's contracts, with regular collection of milk by motor lorry, helped overcome the disadvantages of remoteness.

A field of fodder kale for the dairy cattle kept by F. W. Dennis, who had farms at Cayton and Seamer, and a retail dairy in nearby Scarborough, Yorkshire, late 1930s.

THE POULTRY FARM

KEEPING HENS had always been one of the Cinderella activities of the farm. Farmers had a distaste for poultry that was proverbial. They were prepared to tolerate only a few hens in the farmyard to provide eggs for the house and earn pin money for the farmer's wife. In the 1920s there was a dramatic change, and in ten years the fowl population of England and Wales doubled, from 30.75 million in 1924 to 61.33 million in 1934. Farmers who had despised hens were now happily managing flocks of hundreds, even thousands of birds. So strong was the growth of this branch of farming that by the 1930s the *Farmer and Stockbreeder* was devoting special pages to the poultry-keeper's interests, while a new industry had grown up to supply his needs.

Poultry had a role similar to that of pigs in that they could be accommodated in a wide variety of farming types, large or small, specialist or mixed. Hens could be kept in intensive housing, they could be in extensive free-range flocks, or – the choice of the majority of farmers – they could be managed in a semi-intensive arrangement between those two extremes. Their demands on labour were not extravagant: a modest flock, up to about four hundred birds, could usually be kept on a family farm without the need to hire extra hands.

The small farmer found he could comfortably accommodate a small flock alongside his principal lines, as W. H. Owen did on his 120 acres in Lincolnshire. At the other end of the scale, F. T. White had a farm of 1,000 acres at Overtown, Wroughton, Wiltshire, on which he kept six thousand hens, while John Betts at Manor Farm, Hampstead Norris, Berkshire, had nine thousand hens on a farm of 320 acres; it was basically a mixed farm, but the poultry were the dominant part. Poultry farming on this scale added a new element to the rural landscape, with large fields full of hen houses. Both White and Betts favoured mobile hen houses with slatted floors, which could be moved around the field. White kept his hens mainly on grassland; other farmers would integrate the flock into the arable rotation, turning it out on to wheat stubble. Folding in this fashion was one of the basic means

Opposite:
Penhirst Poultry Farm, Chellaston, Derbyshire, farmed by H. A. Groome, November 1934.

41

Feeding hens in the field on Mr Alexander's farm, North Walsham, Norfolk, 1937.

Essential equipment for raising chickens – one of the many styles of incubator advertised in the catalogues of Harry Hebditch Ltd in the 1920s.

of flock management. The houses were moved every so often to keep the hens clean and the distribution of manure even.

The hen houses with slatted floors were popular, but new manufacturers were offering coops, incubators and other equipment of all types and sizes. For the economy-conscious there were always alternative forms of hen house, such as an old bus.

F. T. White kept Rhode Island Red and White Wyandotte hens.

Harry Hebditch Ltd, of Martock, Somerset, was one of the leading suppliers of hen houses and other equipment for the poultry farmer.

Light Sussex cock
and hen.

These recognised breeds, along with White Leghorn and Light Sussex, took the place of the mongrel barn-door fowl in the farmyard. Cross-bred hens were also popular, especially when techniques in crossing were established in the 1930s that avoided unwanted cockerel chicks. This was a boost to egg producers, and it encouraged the growth of specialist poultry farming.

Most hens were kept for their eggs. Cheap motor transport facilitated this, as for many of the specialised farm products. Regular collections of produce were made by lorries calling at the farms. John Betts had some business in table birds, mainly through Reading market, but he was relatively unusual in that. Chicken was far from being established as part of the nation's diet in the 1930s, and the limited demand for poultry meat was met mainly by ducks and geese.

Some of the large flocks of hens kept by John Betts at Hampstead Norris, Berkshire.

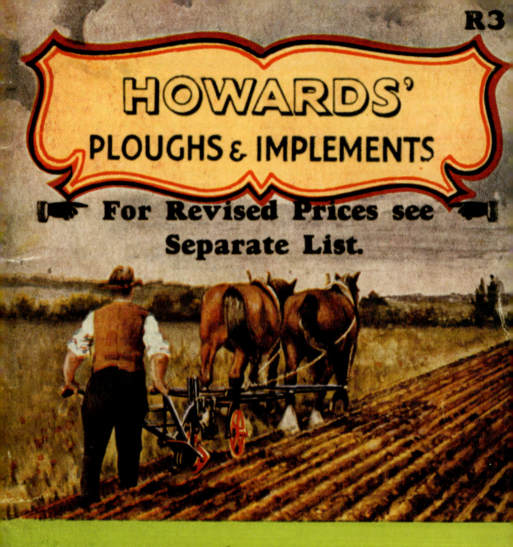

R3

HOWARDS'
PLOUGHS & IMPLEMENTS

☞ For Revised Prices see
Separate List. ☜

Manufactured by

RANSOMES, SIMS &
JEFFERIES LTD

Successors to JAMES & FREDK. HOWARD LTD BEDFORD
(Agricultural Section)

ORWELL WORKS · IPSWICH

H. No. 12625HH. 5H. 3612.

THE ARABLE FARMER

WHILE FARMERS turned to livestock for the bulk of their income, most still had some fields to till: there were still 9 million acres of arable land in England and Wales. About 1.5 million of these were growing wheat. Despite the low prices, there were farmers keeping land under the plough. E. W. K. Slade, president of the National Farmers Union in 1931, was one who had 'maintained his adherence to the gospel of the plough right through the recent trying years', as the *Farmer and Stockbreeder* put it. He had 800 acres of arable land on his farm at Compton in the Berkshire downland, where he had moved in 1908. Barley for malting was his main cereal cash crop. In place of roots, he grew kale and grasses as feed for sheep and the herd of beef cattle. In this way he could maintain much of the tradition of arable farming.

Both Slade and J. W. Pye on his mixed farm in Kent were fortunate in having malting barley as a paying cereal crop. Few farmers found growing cereals worthwhile as cash crops. They could be used as feed for stock, but even so the acreage sown to wheat and barley fell by nearly half during the 1920s. The introduction of a subsidy under the 1932 Wheat Act encouraged farmers to sow wheat again, and its acreage recovered somewhat during the 1930s. The land under oats continued to fall, as the number of horses in town and country declined.

There were a few exceptions to the trend away from cereals. Two brothers, S. E. and J. F. Alley, decided to become specialist low-cost cereal producers. They had a farm of 1,100 acres at South Creake near Fakenham, Norfolk – an area of prime arable land, with soils and climate ideal for growing cereals. They grew just one crop – wheat – sowing two-thirds of their land with it each year. On the remainder they grew lupins or mustard as catch crops to give the land a break. They used artificial fertilisers, as they kept no stock of their own. The Alleys went in for full-blooded mechanisation: no half-way house with a few horses kept alongside the tractors; no making do with their old horse-drawn implements attached to a tractor. They simply had two crawler tractors together with four-furrow ploughs and other implements designed for power farming. They had seed

Opposite:
There was still a demand for horse-drawn farm implements in the 1920s and 1930s, and the leading makers, such as Ransomes (owners of the Howards brand), produced an extensive range.

Binder twine was useful not only for tying the sheaves, but for minor repairs to fences and gates, tying sacks, and numerous other jobs around the farm.

The horseman – with his dog in attendance – about to take the fertiliser distributor out on E. J. Proctor's farm at Bishop's Stortford, Hertfordshire. Behind him is a stack of hay partly cut through to feed the stock.

drills that sowed thirty-three rows, twice the size of horse-drawn drills; using two of them, they could sow 70 acres in a day. They were among the first to buy a combine harvester, in the late 1930s, when there were only a few at work in England. By these means they kept labour requirements to a

minimum: when Pye had twenty-four labourers, the Alleys had only four full-time employees, with three or four casual workers at harvest time. The farmers who had the South Creake farm before the Alley brothers employed as many as thirty men.

Sugar beet was a new crop on the farm of the 1920s. There had been many previous attempts to popularise it in the late nineteenth century. Processing factories had been built, but very few farmers were persuaded of the value of the crop. That took a rare measure of government intervention, with the introduction of the sugar beet subsidy in 1924. It had a dramatic effect: the acreage in England and Wales devoted to the crop rose from 22,000 acres to 223,000 by 1927. The arable counties of eastern England were where most beet was grown. Norfolk alone accounted for a quarter of the total, and the counties from north Essex to Lincolnshire together accounted for more than two-thirds.

Sugar beet proved to be something of a saviour for farmers who were finding it difficult to diversify away from their established pattern of arable

On the Alley brothers' farm in Norfolk a crawler tractor draws a sledge loaded with hay bales, April 1931.

farming. It was invaluable as a root crop that could fit into established arable rotations. It was also a cash crop: growers worked under contract with one of the beet-processing factories established following the introduction of the beet subsidy. There were more than a dozen factories working by 1928, most of them in eastern England, such as Bardney, Brigg, Newark and Wissington. Farmers within a radius of about 25 miles were best placed to gain from growing the crop. The season of the sugar beet harvest was short, concentrated into a few weeks of the autumn. The factories and growers would talk of the year's beet 'campaign' as harvesters and transport were mobilised to get the crop lifted and delivered to the factory.

For many farmers in the eastern counties sugar beet became their most valuable crop. The cereals they grew in their rotation were of subsidiary importance, most likely used for livestock feed. Some farmers had almost a third of their land under roots – a combination of beet and potatoes – so important was beet to them. The beet tops were fed to sheep, and beet pulp, a by-product of the processing, could be used for cattle feed. Growing sugar beet was by and large unmechanised: the first harvesting machines were only just appearing at the end of the 1930s. The absence of machines provided

Sugar beet was a very labour-intensive crop. Harvesting was still done by hand in the 1930s, the roots having to be lifted and the dirt knocked off, often on cold days in late autumn and early winter.

work for the labourers, albeit hard. Lifting and topping beet in the cold days
of late autumn became one of the toughest assignments on the farm.

Clifford Nicholson made his fortune from growing potatoes in
Lincolnshire, the county that was more closely associated with the crop than
any other. Nicholson had started out in farming in 1912, with a tenancy of
500 acres, and had 9,000 acres in 1939. Potatoes had been a crop of the Fens,
but now any farmer would put some land aside for potatoes if he could. The
new snack of potato crisps created an additional market for the crop. Smith's
Potato Crisps Ltd moved in during the 1930s, buying from established
growers, but also taking on a large estate of their own at Nocton,
Lincolnshire.

Potatoes were one of a number of more specialist crops, the arable
equivalent, it might be said, of pigs and poultry. Growing vegetables was
another activity that offered a fair chance of profit, as prices were consistently

Loading sugar beet
at Mrs Love's farm,
Happisburgh,
Norfolk,
November 1935,
for delivery to
the factory.

at or above the average for all farm crops. Demand for fresh vegetables was growing, and a new market was opened up with the rise of canning from nothing to an industry producing about fifty million cans a year by 1930. Arthur Rickwood became known as the 'Carrot King' after he built up a large estate in Cambridgeshire, Suffolk and Norfolk, on which he grew carrots and other vegetables. He had his own washing and grading plant, so that he could supply markets with produce in much the same way as growers dealing with supermarkets do now. Miss Joan Edwards was another who was alive to the need for marketing. She had her own brand name, 'Over the Water', for the Brussels sprouts, beans, parsnips and other vegetables that she sold from her farms in Suffolk.

Rickwood and Edwards were operating on a very large scale, but farmers from Gloucestershire to Norfolk started growing as field crops what had hitherto been mainly the preserve of small market-garden producers. As well as those who specialised in them, vegetables could be taken up by the mixed farmer, as J. W. Pye did in Kent. The effect was that, in all, production of vegetables between 1923 and 1936 increased by 81 per cent. The acreage of

Opposite top: Riddling and grading potatoes from the clamps on the farms of Smith's Potato Crisps in February 1937. A narrow-gauge railway provided transport around the estate.

Opposite bottom: Planting potatoes by hand, Pangbourne, Berkshire.

Below: Hoeing onions by hand in Berkshire.

Riddling and grading Brussels sprouts on one of the farms of Joan Edwards at Bardwell Manor, near Bury St Edmunds, in 1936. The twenty-two-year old managed 5,000 acres for her father and 350 acres on her own account.

T. L. May was a specialist fruit grower at Sproughton, Suffolk. He also grew vegetables, sych as these cabbages being sent out in 1934.

IVYWELL FRUIT FARMS.
SPROUGHTON

carrots and cauliflowers more than doubled in fifteen years, and the acreage of Brussels sprouts increased nearly threefold.

The canning firms that bought crops of peas and beans were also in the market for fruit, though the growing of soft and orchard fruit was more of a niche activity compared with vegetable production. It was a business for the hardier souls as losses could be heavy in a bad year. A respectable amount of capital was needed, as fruit-growing became one of the more scientific of agricultural pursuits. The higher yields that could be achieved as a result could give a worthwhile return, encouraging fruit farmers – and vegetable growers – to be among the first to invest in new machines. In general, however, expansion of fruit production was modest.

Row-crop tractors had narrow wheels to negotiate the inter-row spaces, and were used for work with horticultural crops such as strawberries, as in this view at Ivywell Fruit Farm.

Ransomes

THRASHING MACHINERY

POWER ON THE LAND

T HE FARMER wanted mechanical power, as he had done for the best part of a century. He could – and did – hire the steam engines of the threshing and ploughing contractors, but in the 1920s most of the work on the farm was still done by horses, or by hand. There were still 823,000 horses on the farms of England and Wales.

What the farmer wanted most was a light, versatile and cheap tractor. In the Ivel and Saunderson tractors of the Edwardian years he got more or less that. The post-war Saunderson Model G was a much-improved tractor but, although it was reasonably light and versatile, it was not cheap. Cheapness came from Henry Ford, who was able to mass-produce his Fordson tractor following an order for five thousand from the British government in 1917. They were intended to aid the war effort, but most arrived after the armistice. In 1921 the Fordson sold for £260, comfortably undercutting British-made tractors, such as the Austin at £360 and the British Wallis at £525. The Fordson captured most of the market. Its nearest competitor was the International, especially the 10-20 model, another American product.

Even at £260, price remained an issue with farmers contemplating buying a tractor in the 1920s. The impact of the economic slump after the First World War in reducing farmers' spending power considerably slowed the process of mechanisation during this decade. It was said that many in the 1920s did not replace the tractors supplied to them during the war when they wore out or broke down, going back instead to the horses. Most farmers could afford neither the tractor nor the other implements that might go with it, although there were expedients to which they could resort in adapting existing equipment. Cheap alternatives to the tractor were on the market as well: converted cars, usually the Ford Model T, and lorries, often former military vehicles, all adapted to the role of farm tractor.

The pace of mechanisation increased in the 1930s. Those who had got through the previous decade were often in a better position to invest, while initiatives such as the Wheat Act and the introduction of the marketing boards were providing more secure conditions in which to do so. More interest was

Opposite:
The steam-powered threshing machine had been a feature of farming for about eighty years, but the tractor was taking over during the 1930s. This is the cover of a Ransomes catalogue.

being shown in tractors and machinery, with regular features in *Farmers Weekly* going into the subject in some depth. It was reflected in the statistics: the first census of tractors was carried out in 1937, when there were 43,000 of them in England and Wales. Most were in the arable east of England, especially where land was intensively cultivated. The greatest density of tractors was in the Holland division of Lincolnshire, where the profits earned from growing potatoes and other high-value crops had encouraged investment. Farmers in the Vale of Evesham, another area of intensive horticulture, had also taken to the tractor.

The arrival of the first tractor on the farm was a day of some excitement, still remembered by those alive at that time. Reg Dobbs's father bought his first tractor, a Fordson, in 1938, paying £130 for it. It had taken Mr Dobbs eight years since entering his farm of 120 acres in the Fens to build up sufficient funds to buy the tractor and additional equipment such as the cultivator. The day of the tractor's arrival was a red-letter day, marking the farm's first big step into the modern world.

Tractors such as the Fordson had their foibles – getting them to start could be an art in itself – but in general they were simple to operate. The horseman was usually given the task of driving the new tractor, and, after remembering to use the brake rather than shouting 'whoa!' to stop it, he was soon in full command.

Shortage of capital was still holding most farmers back from investment, with the result that few went wholesale into mechanisation. Most worked with a combination of tractor and horse power, even on large farms. F. P. Chamberlain, with 500 acres at Crowmarsh, Oxfordshire, bought his first tractors in 1927, but retained several horses, which he continued

Left: The International 10-20 tractor was second in popularity to the Fordson during this period. This poster shows it with a binder.

Opposite top: The post-war Saunderson Model G tractor.

Opposite bottom: A Ransomes three-furrow tractor plough illustrated on the cover of a 1930s catalogue.

to use. Edward Lousley, the manager of the 4,000-acre Lockinge estate, now in Oxfordshire, had eleven tractors at work by 1935, but much of the work was still done by horses. Some farmers wanted to keep their options open, not convinced that the tractor was right for every job. J. W. Pye in Kent was of that view, believing that tractors should be rested through the wet months of winter, when they might harm the land.

Shortage of funds meant that there was still a great deal of make-do-and-mend, for, having got the tractor, the farmer could not always afford the implements designed specifically for it. He had plenty of choice, as implement manufacturers produced multi-furrow ploughs with self-lift mechanism, seed

Left: Massey-Harris and Blackstone had a joint marketing agreement in the 1930s, and this catalogue cover illustrates a Massey-Harris tractor with a power binder.

57

Growing grass for cattle feed prompted the development of new implements. The 'Cutlift' grass-cutter was a 1930s precursor of the modern forage harvester, cutting and loading grass into a trailer.

One money-saving expedient was to adapt old cars for field work. This is the Cole lifting car hay sweep, driven by its designer, Mr Cole. The car is a Durrant bought for £1.

drills to sow far more rows than a horse-drawn machine could, and power binders designed to work from the power take-off on the tractor (a mechanism introduced in 1926). Until he could afford these, the farmer often converted his existing implements for use with the tractor, usually by the simple method of cutting off the horse shafts and fixing a tractor drawbar in their place.

There were exceptions – farmers who converted their farms entirely to mechanical power. H. J. Hosier, the dairy farmer in Wiltshire, argued that a

tractor working for sixteen hours a day could get 60 acres ploughed and drilled with oats in just four days. Even paying the men extra to work the shifts required saved in the longer term, both on total labour bills, and by getting the crop in on time. The Alley brothers in Norfolk spent £3,400 on modernising the equipment on their 1,100-acre farm. For that they bought two big crawler tractors – 40-hp Caterpillars – together with tractor ploughs, big seed drills and other implements. The Alleys were among the first to buy a combine harvester – in fact two, made by Massey-Harris, with a cutting width of 12 feet. Roland Dudley, at Linkenholt, Hampshire, was another pioneer with the combine harvester, and, like the Alleys, thoroughgoing in the mechanisation of his farming.

The combine harvester was introduced to Britain in 1928, but it was expensive and needed large fields in which to operate, so only a few of those farming on a large scale were able to make use of it. The combines of the 1930s – Case, International, Massey-Harris – were all imported from North America. There were fewer than a hundred at work in the whole of Britain in 1939.

At the end of the 1930s the farms of England and Wales were far more mechanised than they had been at the beginning of the 1920s. Tractors and powered machines were no longer only for the enthusiasts and those farming on the largest scale. These machines were saving manpower and horse power, but, with 549,000 horses still working on farms in 1939, mechanisation still had a long way to go.

A Deering combine harvester at work on the farm of D. T. Slade in Hertfordshire, August 1938. The greater power of a crawler tractor was useful for hauling these machines.

RETURN TO WAR

THE HORSES still at work would have been one of a number of features that an Edwardian farmer returning to his farm in 1939 would have found familiar among what he saw in the fields, the crops and the livestock. But a great deal had changed, and there were things he would not have recognised in the way his successors were farming, such as the place accorded to chickens and pigs, and the new tractor-driven machines.

The changes of the 1920s and 1930s were, however, but a prelude to what was to come in the Second World War and its aftermath. Some of the developments of the late 1930s were in anticipation of future war, as ministries started to put in place much of the administrative machinery needed to manage a wartime farming industry. Measures had already been introduced to encourage arable farming, notably the 1937 Agriculture Act. This brought in new price guarantees for barley and oats, increased a subsidy for wheat introduced in 1932, subsidised fertilisers, and made grants for land drainage. The Act was not overtly a wartime measure but a recognition of agriculture's need for support.

The government was certainly mindful of events in Europe, and was acting closely upon the recommendations of a departmental committee of 1935–6 investigating the question of food supply in time of war. The need for agriculture to be in a better state of productiveness in a case of national emergency was a major consideration of that body. A number of measures were implemented to help that process: county war agricultural committees were set up in readiness and so was the Women's Land Army. The Government was determined that there should be an immediate response should there be a war – no waiting two or three years while farmers responded to market trends and appeals to patriotism.

So it was that when war was declared in September 1939, the Ministry of Agriculture was more prepared than it had been in 1914. The stage was set for a major transformation of English farming, as the orders to plough up large tracts of the grassland upon which the inter-war farm had been based were quickly issued.

Opposite:
Deering was one
of the constituents
of the
International
Harvester
Corporation of
America. This is an
advertising leaflet
for their tractor
binder of 1938.

Ploughing with horses on heavy soil in Leicestershire, 1936.

The British-built Ferguson tractor of 1936 introduced the principle of hydraulic power transmission to the implements. One is seen with a binder on T. Warne's farm at Shalford, Surrey, in August 1937.

FURTHER READING

Beard, M. *English Landed Society in the Twentieth Century*. Routledge, 1989.

Bensusan, S. L. *Latter-day Rural England*. Benn, 1928.

Brassley, Paul; Burchardt, Jeremy; and Thompson, Lynne (editors). *The English Countryside between the Wars: Regeneration or Decline?* Boydell Press, 2006.

Brendon, P. *The Dark Valley: A Panorama of the 1930s*. Knopf, 2000.

Brown, Jonathan. *The Edwardian Farm*. Shire, 2010.

Cherrington, J. *On the Smell of an Oily Rag: My 50 Years in Farming*. Northwood Books, 1979.

Dobbs, Reg. *The Oldest Young Farmer: the life of a Lincolnshire farmer*. Sutton, 2007.

Dudgeon, P. *Village Voices: A Portrait of Change in England's Green and Pleasant Land 1915–1990*. Sidgwick & Jackson, 1989.

Gardiner, Juliet. *The Thirties: An Intimate History*. Harper Press, 2010.

Martin, John. *The Development of Modern Agriculture: British Farming since 1931*. Macmillan, 2000.

Perren, R. *Agriculture in Depression 1870–1940*. Cambridge University Press, 1995.

Street, A. G. *Farmer's Glory*. Faber & Faber, 1934.

Whetham, Edith H. *The Agrarian History of England and Wales, volume VIII, 1914–1939*. Cambridge University Press, 1978.

Williamson, Henry. *The Story of a Norfolk Farm*. Faber & Faber, 1940.

An International tractor tows a tined cultivator.

INDEX

Page numbers in italics refer to illustrations